UNDERSTANDING ASTHMA

HEALTH MATTERS

BY HOLLY DUHIG

PowerKiDS press™

New York

Published in 2019 by The Rosen Publishing Group
29 East 21st Street, New York, NY 10010

Copyright © 2018 Booklife Publishing
This edition is published by arrangement with Booklife Publishing

Edited by: Kristy Holmes
Designed by: Drue Rintoul

Image Credits

All images are courtesy of Shutterstock.com, unless otherwise specified. With thanks to Getty Images, Thinkstock Photo and iStockphoto.
Front Cover – sirtravelalot. 2 – bubutu. 4&5 – Image Point Fr, Lopolo. 6&7 – Zdorov Kirill Vladimirovich, Africa Studio, Ugorenkov Aleksandr, CHIEW. 8&9 – absolutimages, MANDY GODBEHEAR, all_about_people. 10&11 – Danielle Jones (BookLife). 12&13 – Orawan Pattarawimonchai, Africa Studio. 14&15 – Orawan Pattarawimonchai, Arvind Balaraman. 16&17 – sirtravelalot, Sebastian Kaulitzki, MJTH. 18&19 – Hung Chung Chih, Dagmara_K. 20&21 – Fotokostic, Tinseltown, Photo Works, By Ash Carter (151119-D-1X214-004) [CC BY 2.0 (http://creativecommons.org/licenses/by/2.0)], via Wikimedia Commons. 22&23 – Lopolo, Lauren Simmons. 24&25 – wavebreakmedia, sirtravelalot. 26&27 – MaeManee, Lopolo. 28&29 – LightField Studios, Monkey Business Images. 30 – Monkey Business Images.

Cataloging-in-Publication Data

Names: Duhig, Holly.
Title: Understanding asthma / Holly Duhig.
Description: New York : PowerKids Press, 2019. | Series: Health matters | Includes glossary and index.
Identifiers: LCCN ISBN 9781538338476 (pbk.) | ISBN 9781538338469 (library bound) | ISBN 9781538338483 (6 pack)
Subjects: LCSH: Asthma--Juvenile literature. | Asthma in children--Juvenile literature.
Classification: LCC RC591.D84 2019 | DDC 618.92'238--dc23

Manufactured in the United States of America

CPSIA Compliance Information: Batch CSPK18: For further information, contact Rosen Publishing, New York, New York, at 1-800-237-9932.

CONTENTS

Words that look like **this** are explained in the glossary on page 31.

WHAT IS ASTHMA?

Asthma is a lung disease. It is a chronic disease, which means it affects people all their lives and can never be completely cured. Asthma causes **symptoms** such as shortness of breath, wheezing, coughing, a tight feeling in your chest, and sometimes a **severe** flare-up, called an asthma attack.

An asthma attack happens when the airways in your lungs suddenly narrow. This makes breathing very difficult. With modern medicine, asthma can be treated so that it is manageable, and people with asthma can live long, active, and healthy lives.

FACT

ASTHMA AFFECTS BOTH ADULTS AND CHILDREN.
1 IN 10 CHILDREN IN THE U.S. HAVE ASTHMA.

Asthma is quite common and affects both children and adults. More than 300 million people in the world have asthma. Some people have mild asthma that does not affect them very often and is easily controlled. Others have more severe asthma which is less easily controlled and brought on by many different triggers. Triggers are things that can make asthma worse or cause someone to have a flare-up or attack. They are things such as dust, smoke, aerosol sprays, cold weather, and catching a cold or the flu.

WHY DO SOME PEOPLE GET ASTHMA ?

It is not always clear why some people get asthma and some don't. Asthma is not contagious, which means you can't catch asthma from someone who has it. It can be **genetic**, which means that if your parent or close family member has asthma, you are more likely to have it, too.

DUST MASKS, LIKE THE ONE THIS MAN IS WEARING, CAN HELP PROTECT THE LUNGS AGAINST ASTHMA TRIGGERS.

Sometimes, adults develop asthma after working in places with lots of asthma triggers for a long time. For example, painters and builders sometimes develop asthma because the tiny particles in paint and dust can irritate their lungs. If this happens over a long time, they can develop asthma.

If someone has symptoms of asthma they will usually go to see a doctor who will do lots of tests. A doctor might look at your eyes, ears, nose, mouth, and skin to make sure that you are not suffering from an illness or sickness bug. Then they might do some tests on your lungs. You may be asked to breathe into a spirometer, which is a device that tests how much air you are able to breathe in and out and how fast you are able to do this. Another device, called a peak flow meter, might be used to test how quickly you can force air out of your lungs. You will be asked by your doctor to breathe into this device as hard and fast as you can.

PEAK FLOW METER

SPIROMETER

FACT

IF SOMEONE IS DIAGNOSED WITH ASTHMA THEY WILL USUALLY HAVE AN ASTHMA NURSE, WHOSE JOB IT IS TO HELP THEM TO CONTROL THEIR ASTHMA.

SYMPTOMS AND TRIGGERS

The main symptoms of asthma are:

WHEEZING

This happens when air passing through the narrow airways in your lungs creates a whistling sound.

TIGHT CHEST

This can feel like your lungs are being squashed and is caused by the tightening of muscles around your lungs.

COUGHING

This symptom can be brought on by having too much **mucus** in your lungs or by certain triggers.

An asthma attack might lead to other symptoms too, such as dizziness – caused by not enough oxygen getting to your brain – and a fast heartbeat. These symptoms are often made worse by the panic and worry that can come with having an asthma attack.

There are two types of asthma. Allergic asthma is brought on by triggers that cause an allergic reaction. Nonallergic asthma is brought on by different triggers.

Triggers that cause an allergic reaction are called allergens. People can be allergic to all sorts of things, from peanuts to penicillin. Allergens that cause asthma tend to be airborne. This means that they travel through the air and can be breathed in. A common airborne allergen is pollen, the fine powdery substance made by flowers and trees. Being allergic to pollen is called having hay fever and can cause symptoms such as a runny nose and itchy eyes. The difference between someone with hay fever and someone with allergic asthma is that in someone with asthma, breathing in pollen causes asthma symptoms.

OTHER AIRBORNE ALLERGENS INCLUDE DUST, MOLD, AND ANIMAL DANDER.

WHAT CAUSES ASTHMA SYMPTOMS **?**

Asthma symptoms are caused by inflammation in your lungs, making it difficult for air to pass through. Your lungs are a pair of spongy organs you use to breathe. You breathe in oxygen, a gas that all animals need in order to survive, and you breathe out a waste gas called carbon dioxide. Just as a car needs gas, your body needs oxygen to fuel it. Your lungs are made from a huge system of airways called bronchi and bronchioles that deliver oxygen to your body. At the end of the bronchioles are the alveoli, which transfer the oxygen to the blood so it can be carried around the body. They also take carbon dioxide out of the blood which you then breathe out.

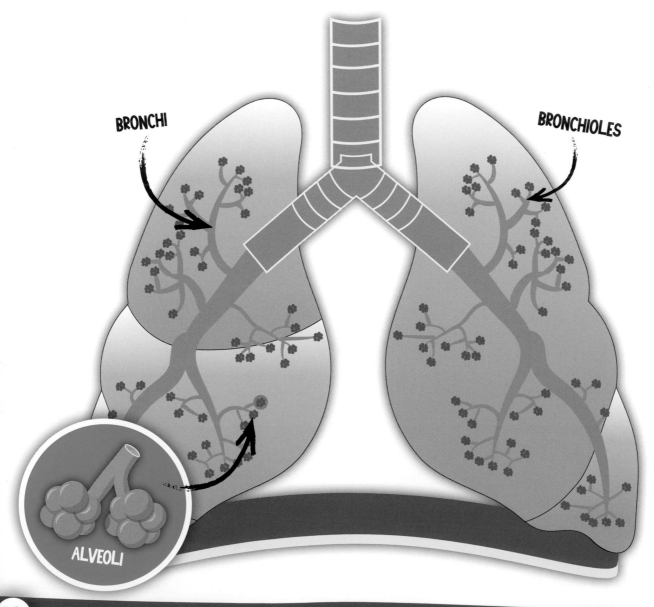

BRONCHI

BRONCHIOLES

ALVEOLI

How Asthma Affects the Lungs

Asthma causes the lining of your airways, called the mucosal lining, to become inflamed and swell up. This makes the airways much narrower than they should be. Bronchi and bronchioles are also wrapped in rings of muscle that **contract** when exposed to asthma triggers. Asthma triggers also cause the mucosal lining to produce a sticky mucus which further blocks the airways. Narrow airways mean less air can get in and out of the lungs. This can make a person with asthma feel as if they are breathing through a straw. Not getting enough air can be very dangerous. Humans can't go without air for very long.

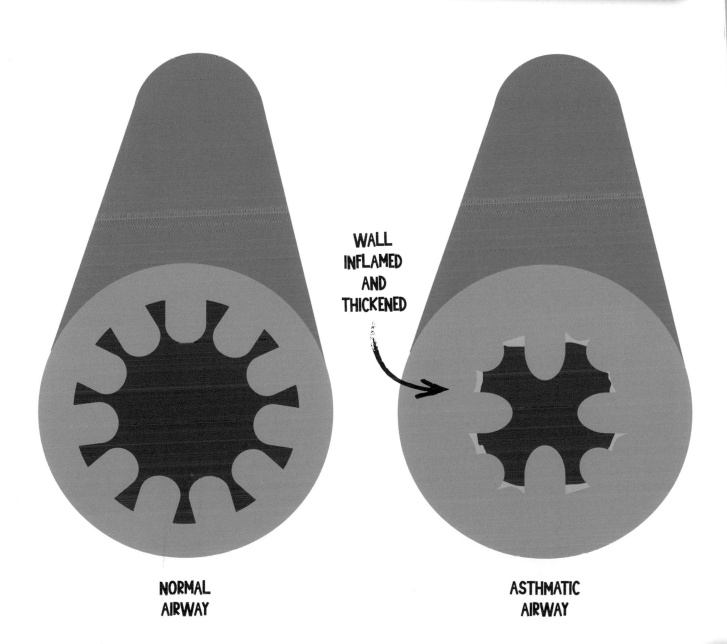

WALL INFLAMED AND THICKENED

NORMAL AIRWAY

ASTHMATIC AIRWAY

TREATING ASTHMA: INHALERS

Preventer Inhalers

There are two main types of inhalers used to treat asthma: preventer inhalers and reliever inhalers. Preventer inhalers are used to control asthma symptoms. Reliever inhalers, on the other hand, can be used during an asthma attack.

Preventer inhalers are usually brown, red, or orange, and people with asthma may need to use these every day. This type of inhaler contains drugs called steroids which are anti-inflammatory, meaning they reduce the swelling in the lungs. Steroids are also used in some nasal sprays that treat blocked noses caused by colds or allergies because they help reduce swelling in the blood vessels in the back of the nose.

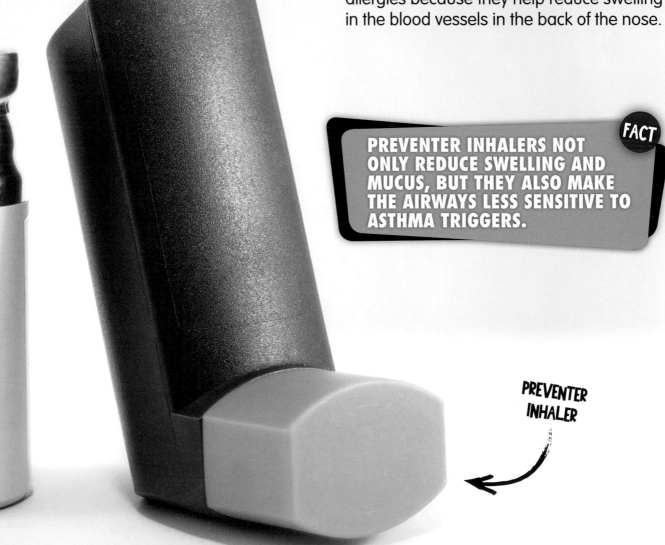

FACT

PREVENTER INHALERS NOT ONLY REDUCE SWELLING AND MUCUS, BUT THEY ALSO MAKE THE AIRWAYS LESS SENSITIVE TO ASTHMA TRIGGERS.

PREVENTER INHALER

Reliever Inhalers

Reliever inhalers tend to be blue and they are used in emergencies to relieve strong asthma symptoms and attacks. You might also hear them being called bronchodilators (bron-co-die-lay-tors) because they **dilate** the bronchi and bronchioles in your lungs. Instead of steroids, most reliver inhalers use a drug called albuterol (also called salbutamol or Ventolin) which helps to relax the muscles that surround your airways, making them wider. The body reacts to these drugs much more quickly than it reacts to steroids which is why they are used for emergencies. Reliever inhalers shouldn't need to be used very often, so if you have asthma and are needing to use your reliever inhaler more often than your doctor or asthma nurse says you should, it is a sign that your asthma is not as well controlled as it could be.

FACT

SOME PEOPLE WHO PLAY A LOT OF SPORTS USE THEIR RELIEVER INHALER BEFORE STARTING EXERCISE.

Types of Inhaler Devices

METERED DOSE INHALERS:

These are one of the most commonly used inhalers and they work by spraying asthma medicine as a mist when you press a button. Some people find these types of inhalers take a bit of getting used to because you have to make sure you have already started taking a breath when you press the button. You must also make sure to aim the spray at the back of the throat so it gets into your lungs and does not hit the roof of your mouth.

DRY POWDER INHALER:

Instead of a mist, these devices deliver medicine to the lungs in the form of dry powder. These tend to be breath-activated, which means there is no button to press and they simply release the medicine when you put them to your mouth and breathe in. Dry powder inhalers are often shaped like a disk and have a lever that controls the **dose** of medicine.

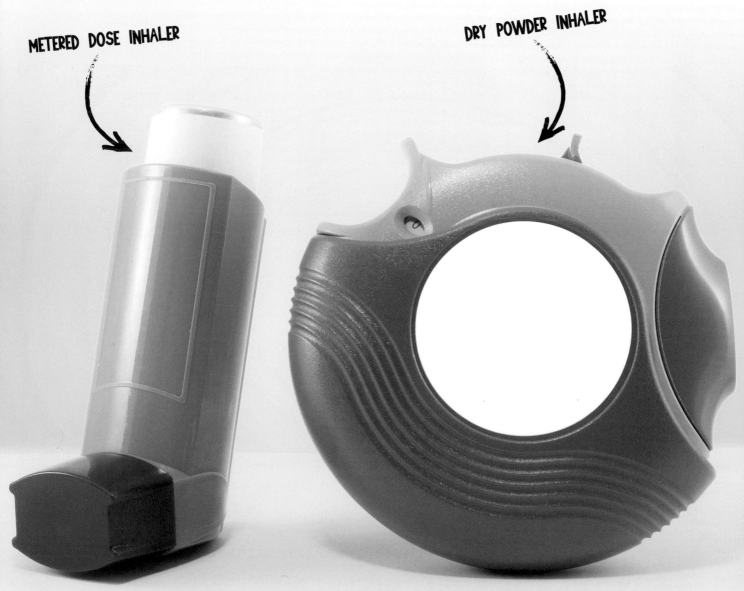

METERED DOSE INHALER

DRY POWDER INHALER

INHALERS COME IN ALL DIFFERENT SHAPES AND SIZES. SOME LOOK LIKE TUBES WHILE OTHERS LOOK LIKE FLAT DISKS.

Spacers

Spacers are large, plastic devices which are sometimes attached to a mask. You can put your inhaler on one end of the device and use the over-mouth mask to breathe in the medicine. These are useful because they make sure none of the medicine escapes and they allow you to breathe it in more slowly. However, they are quite big so children with asthma often use smaller inhaler devices when they are out and about.

IT IS IMPORTANT TO CLEAN YOUR SPACER REGULARLY. SOAK IT FOR 15 MINUTES IN WARM WATER, AND CLEAN IT WITH DISH SOAP, BUT DONT SCRUB THE INSIDE. GET A NEW SPACER AT LEAST EVERY YEAR. GOOD HYGIENE WILL STOP GERMS FROM GETTING INTO YOUR LUNGS.

If you have been given a reliever inhaler by your asthma nurse, it is important that you remember to keep it with you at all times. You must always remember to bring it with you when you go to school, when you go over to a friend's house, and even when you go on vacation. It is dangerous to have an asthma attack and not have your inhaler with you.

CASE STUDY: BECKY

My name is Becky and I have asthma. I have had asthma ever since I can remember so I'm very used to dealing with it, but I still have to use my preventer inhaler every day to make sure I don't get a flare-up. If I do get a flare-up, I go to see my asthma nurse who helps me come up with a plan to manage my asthma. It usually only gets bad when I am sick because sickness bugs can affect your lungs. I usually go to my doctor and get a flu **vaccination** every year which helps my body to protect me from flu viruses.

FACT

GETTING INFLUENZA OR "THE FLU" CAN PUT PEOPLE WITH ASTHMA MORE AT RISK OF GETTING LUNG INFECTIONS SUCH AS PNEUMONIA (NEW-MO-NEE-A).

I have allergic asthma which means lots of different things can set off my asthma symptoms, especially dust. Dust sets off my symptoms because I'm allergic to the tiny creatures that live in dust, called dust mites. They like to live in soft things like carpets, bedsheets, and even cuddly toys. Because of this, we don't have carpets in our house; we have tiles instead, which we vacuum often. My mom and dad also wash my soft toys in hot water to kill all the mites that like to hide in them.

DUST MITES ARE
MICROSCOPIC.

OTHER WAYS OF TREATING ASTHMA

Inhalers and medication are great for treating asthma but there are lots of other things that can be done to help keep asthma under control. Like Becky, many people with asthma have to make sure the **fabrics** in their house are nice and clean. Washing and vacuuming carpets and curtains can help get rid of asthma triggers like dust mites. Sometimes people need to do decorating or building work on their house. People with asthma might have to avoid being at home when building work is being done.

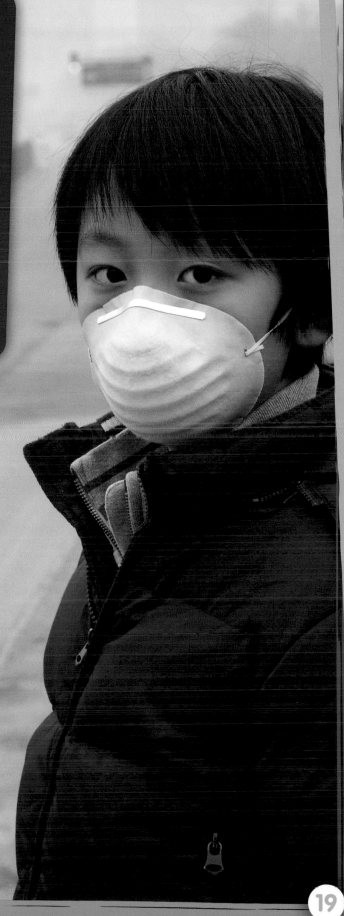

Air Pollution

Air pollution is when harmful gases are released into the air by things like **power stations**, factories, and fumes from cars, boats, and airplanes. Natural things such as fires, volcanic eruptions, and extreme weather such as hurricanes can also cause air pollution. Air pollution levels have risen by eight percent globally in the past five years and are getting worse. People with asthma often have to be more careful to avoid **pollutants** such as smog, bonfires, and cigarette smoke.

MANY PEOPLE WHO LIVE IN BIG CITIES WEAR MASKS TO PROTECT THEIR LUNGS FROM AIR POLLUTION.

EXERCISE

Although it can trigger asthma symptoms, exercise can be really important in helping control asthma in the long term. Exercise can actually help to strengthen your heart and lungs and build their **stamina** and **capacity**. Many children with asthma worry that their condition will mean they can't take part in sports like other children, but this isn't true.

When exercising with asthma, it is important that you always have your reliever inhaler close by. In winter, when the weather is cold, the shock of the temperature change can narrow the airways in the lungs so it can help to stick to indoor activities, but if you remember to dress warm you can exercise outdoors, too.

Having asthma doesn't mean you are weak or unfit, it just means that you need to take slightly more care of your lungs than other people might. Asthma is a manageable condition, which means it shouldn't stop you from taking part in sports. In fact, some of the most famous athletes in the world have asthma, including famous soccer player David Beckham, Super Bowl champion Jerome Bettis, and three-time gold medalist track and field athlete Jackie Joyner-Kersee.

JACKIE JOYNER-KERSEE

DAVID BECKHAM

JEROME BETTIS

CASE STUDY: DOM

My name is Dominic, or Dom for short, and I had an asthma attack last year in the summer while playing soccer. When it happened I was really scared and I didn't understand why I couldn't breathe properly. My ribs felt really tight and I just couldn't get enough air into my chest. This made me panic which made it much worse. I wanted to cry but my lungs wouldn't let me. Luckily, my coach called for an ambulance to take me to the hospital where they gave me medicine to help me breathe again.

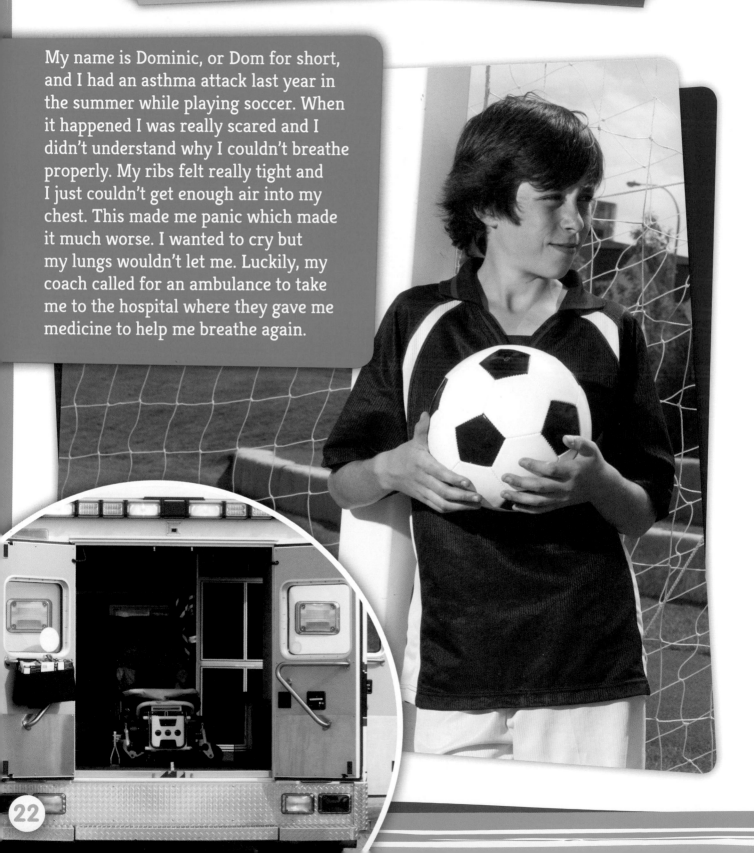

For a long time I was scared to play soccer again. Going near the field just reminded me of having an asthma attack and how scary it was, and made me feel breathless all over again. I told this to my asthma nurse and he was very kind. He told me there was no need to worry so much about having another attack because my asthma can now be treated with my preventer and reliever inhaler. He also gave me some relaxation tips and breathing techniques to use to calm myself down if I start to feel breathless.

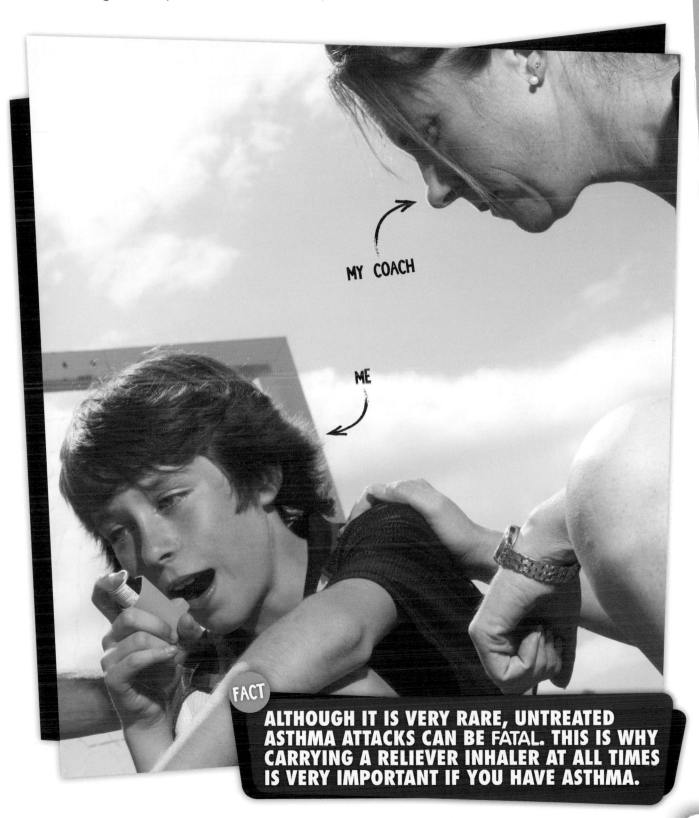

MY COACH

ME

FACT

ALTHOUGH IT IS VERY RARE, UNTREATED ASTHMA ATTACKS CAN BE FATAL. THIS IS WHY CARRYING A RELIEVER INHALER AT ALL TIMES IS VERY IMPORTANT IF YOU HAVE ASTHMA.

KEEPING CALM

Keeping calm during an asthma attack can be difficult because one of the best ways of relaxing – taking deep breaths – might be impossible. Instead, if you can, it is best to try to slow your breathing. When you panic, your body thinks you are in danger and tells your lungs to work harder and faster so you can fight or run away from danger, but this isn't helpful when your lungs are struggling. Slowing your breathing will help calm your brain and allow your lungs to recover on their own. Make sure to sit nice and upright so that you are not squashing your lungs by leaning forward.

It can be difficult to calm yourself down when you feel scared. If you think you are having an asthma attack, find an adult right away. If you can, tell them what is happening. Make sure you are not on your own. An adult can find your inhaler and help you to calm your breathing. Sit up straight, loosen any clothing that is tight around your stomach or chest, and try to think calmly. Remember that your body is strong and you will get through the attack. Take your inhaler as your asthma nurse showed you. While it gets to work, try counting slowly in your head, or focus on something in front of you to help you stay calm.

FACT

IF YOUR RELIEVER INHALER DOESN'T SEEM TO BE HELPING, CALL FOR MEDICAL HELP RIGHT AWAY. IF YOUR RELIEVER WORKS, YOU SHOULD FEEL BETTER, BUT SHOULD STILL SEE YOUR DOCTOR AS SOON AS POSSIBLE.

HOSPITAL TREATMENT

Some people have mild asthma that never gives them an attack, while for others it is more severe. This means that, sometimes, people with asthma will need to go to the hospital. This can feel quite sudden and scary, but there is no need to worry. Ambulances and hospitals are not scary and they are, in fact, the best places to be in an emergency. They have lots of doctors and special equipment that can help you to feel better as quickly as possible.

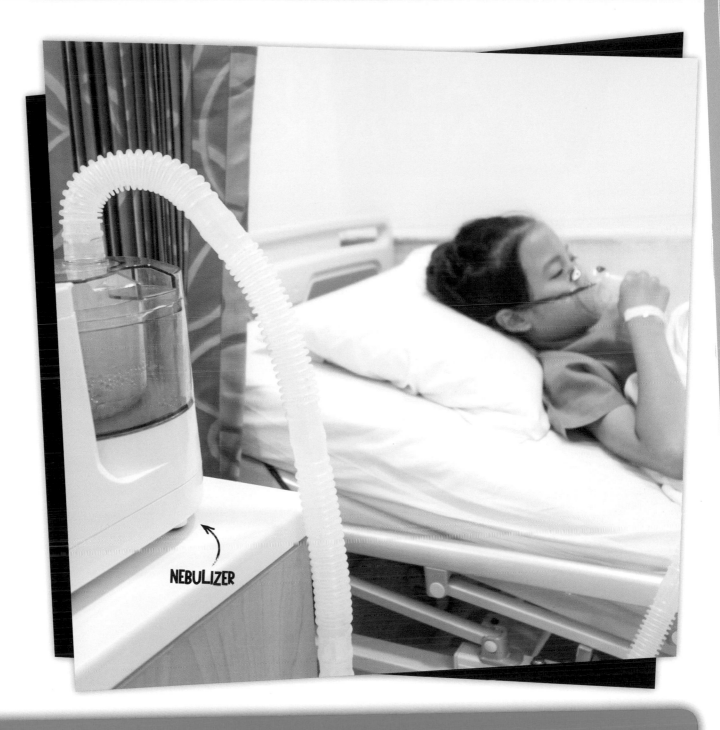

NEBULIZER

In an emergency, **paramedics** might come in an ambulance to help you. Ambulances and hospitals will have a machine called a nebulizer which changes liquid medicine into a breathable mist. This mist can be breathed in through a mask. Nebulizers use medicine that is similar to, but stronger than, what you would have in an inhaler. You might have to stay overnight at a hospital so that doctors can make sure you are fully recovered before letting you go home. Family and friends can come and visit you in the hospital and they might bring you things from home like toys, books, and a change of clothes.

ASTHMA ATTACKS

If someone you are with has an asthma attack, it is important to know what to do. The person having the asthma attack might not be able to tell you what they need because they will be struggling to breathe. Look to see if they have an inhaler with them in their pocket or in their bag.

If they have a metered dose inhaler, you can shake the inhaler and remove the cap for them. You should give them the inhaler and then find an adult. If the person doesn't have an inhaler, make sure to do this right away. An adult will know what to do and when to call for an ambulance.

FACT

IN THE UNLIKELY EVENT THAT THERE IS NO ONE ELSE AROUND, YOU CAN CALL FOR AN AMBULANCE YOURSELF. EVEN IF YOU CAN'T SPEAK, STAY ON THE LINE AND THEY WILL FIND YOU.

LIVING WITH ASTHMA

Living with asthma can be difficult at times. Unlike other children, children with asthma have to learn to be responsible for their medicine even though they are still quite young. This can feel unfair at times and can take some getting used to. However, with the help of parents, caregivers, teachers, and nurses you can learn how to take care of yourself and keep your asthma under control.

People with asthma can live active and healthy lives despite their symptoms. They might simply have to be more careful than others about avoiding allergens and other triggers. Although asthma never completely goes away, many children grow out of some asthma symptoms as they get older. By the time they are adults their asthma symptoms may not affect them as much, or hardly at all.

Having a healthy diet and doing plenty of exercise is the best way to keep your lungs strong and, as long as asthma is well controlled, it doesn't have to stop you from doing all the things you want to do.

GLOSSARY

capacity — how much something can hold

contract — become shorter or smaller

dilate — become larger, wider, or more open

dose — the quantity of a medicine or drug that needs to be taken at a particular time

fabrics — materials made by weaving threads of cotton, wool, nylon, silk, or other threads

fatal — able to cause death

genetic — something passed from a parent to their offspring via genes

microscopic — so small it cannot be seen with the naked eye

mucus — a slimy substance that helps to protect and lubricate certain parts of the human body

paramedics — people trained to give emergency medical care

pneumonia — lung inflammation caused by bacterial or viral infection

pollutants — substances that are harmful or poisonous to the environment

power stations — places that make and send electricity

severe — very bad, serious, or intense

stamina — ability to maintain physical or mental effort

symptoms — things that happen in the body suggesting that there is a disease or disorder

vaccination — treatments designed to make someone immune to a certain disease

INDEX